Pop Hits
Backing Tracks
Kylie

Wise Publications
part of The Music Sales Group
London / New York / Paris / Sydney / Copenhagen / Berlin / Madrid / Tokyo

Published by

Wise Publications

8/9 Frith Street, London W1D 3JB, England.

Exclusive distributors:

Music Sales Limited

8/9 Frith Street, London W1D 3JB, England.

Music Sales Pty Limited

120 Rothschild Avenue, Rosebery, NSW 2018, Australia.

Order No. AM977207

ISBN 1-84449-036-X

Compiled by Lucy Holliday.

Cover designed by Michael Bell Design.

Photographs courtesy of LFI.

Backing vocals by Elly Barnes.

Backing tracks arranged by Danny G, Tim Shaw and CN Productions.

Printed in the United Kingdom.

1. Better The Devil You Know

Words & Music by Mike Stock, Matt Aitken & Pete Waterman

Better the devil you know,
Better the devil you know.

Better the devil you know,
Better the devil you know.
(Oh, oh, oh)

Say you won't leave me no more,
I'll take you back again
No more excuses no, no
'Cause I've heard them all before,
A hundred times or more.

I'll forgive, and forget
If you say you'll never go
'Cause it's true what they say,
It's better the devil you know.

(Oh, oh, oh)

Our love wasn't perfect I know,
I think I know the score.
If you say you love me, oh boy
I can't ask for more,
I'll come if you should call.

I'll forgive, and forget
If you say you'll never go
'Cause it's true what they say,
It's better the devil you know.
I'll be here every day,
Waiting for your love to show.
Yes it's true what they say
It's better the devil you know.

(Oh, oh, oh)

I'll take you back,
I'll take you back again,
I'll take you back,
I'll take you back again.

Say you won't leave me no more,
I'll take you back again
No more excuses no, no
'Cause I've heard them all before,
A hundred times or more.

I'll forgive, and forget
If you say you'll never go
'Cause it's true what they say,
It's better the devil you know.
I'll be here every day,
Waiting for your love to show.
Yes it's true what they say
It's better the devil you know.

repeat to fade

2. Can't Get You Out Of My Head

Words & Music by Cathy Dennis & Rob Davis

La la la,
La la la la la
La la la
La la la la la,
La la la,
La la la la la
La la la
La la la (la la,)

I just can't get you out of my head
Boy your loving is all I think about
I just can't get you out of my head
Boy it's more than I dare to think about.

La la la,
La la la la la
La la la
La la la (la la,)

I just can't get you out of my head
Boy your loving is all I think about
I just can't get you out of my head
Boy it's more than I dare to think about.

Every night,
Every day,
Just to be there in your arms.
Won't you stay?
Won't you lay?
Stay forever and ever and ever and ever...

La la la,
La la la la la
La la la
La la la la la,
La la la,
La la la la la
La la la
La la la (la la.)

I just can't get you out of my head
Boy your loving is all I think about
I just can't get you out of my head
Boy it's more than I dare to think about.

There's a dark secret in me,
Don't leave me locked in your heart.
Set me free,
Feel the need in me.
Set me free,
Stay forever and ever and ever and ever...

La la la,
La la la la la
La la la
La la la la la,
La la la,
La la la la la
La la la
La la la (la la.)

I just can't get you out of my head,
I just can't get you out of my head,
I just can't get you out of my head.

repeat ad lib. to fade

3. Come Into My World

Words & Music by Cathy Dennis & Rob Davis

Come, come, come into my world
Won't you lift me up, up, high up on your love.

Take these arms that were made for lovin'
And this heart that will beat for two,
Take these eyes that were meant for watching over you.
And I've been such a long time waiting,
For someone I could call my own
I've been chasing the life I'm dreaming,
Now I'm home.

I need your love
Like night needs morning.

So won't you, come, come, come into my world
Won't you lift me up, up, high up on your love.
Oh baby come, come, come into my world
Won't you lift me up, up, high up on your, high up on your...

Na, na, na, na, na, na, na, na, na, na, na, na, na
Na, na, na, na, na, na, na.

Take these lips that were made for kissing
And this heart that will see you through,
And these hands that were made to touch and feel you.

So free your love,
Hear me I'm calling.

Oh won't you come, come, come into my world
Won't you lift me up, up, high up on your love
Oh baby, come, come, come into my world
Won't you lift me up, up, high up on your, high up on your...

Na, na, na, na, na, na, na, na, na, na, na, na, na
Na, na, na, na, na, na, na,
Na, na, na, na, na, na, na, na, na, na, na, na, na
Na, na, na, na, na, na, na,

I need your love,
Like night needs morning.

Oh won't you come, come, come into my world
Won't you lift me up, up, high up on your love
Oh baby, come, come, come into my world
Won't you lift me up, up, high up on your, high up on your love.

Na, na, na, na, na, na, na, na, na, na, na, na, na
Na, na, na, na, na, na, na
Na, na, na, na, na, na, na, na, na, na, na, na, na
Na, na, na, na, na, na, na

repeat chorus to fade

4. **Confide In Me**

Words & Music by Steve Anderson, Dave Seaman & Owain Barton

I stand in the distance,
I view from afar.
Should I offer some assistance?
Should it matter, who you are?

We all get hurt by love,
And we all have our cross to bear,
But in the name of understanding now,
A problem should be shared.

Confide in me,
Confide in me.

I can keep a secret,
And throw away the key.
But sometimes to release it
Is to set our children free.

We all get hurt by love,
And we all have our cross to bear,
But in the name of understanding now,
A problem should be shared.

Confide in me,
Confide in me.
Confide in me,
Confide in me.

Violin Solo

Stick or twist,
The choice is yours.
Hit or miss,
What's mine is yours.
Stick or twist,
The choice is yours.
Hit or miss,
What's mine is yours.

We all get hurt by love,
And we all have our cross to bear.
But in the name of understanding now,
A problem should be shared.

Confide in me,
Confide in me.
Confide in me,
Confide in me.

repeat to fade

5. **Especially For You**

Words & Music by Mike Stock, Matt Aitken & Pete Waterman

(Kylie)
Especially for you
I wanna let you know
What I was going through,
All the time we were apart I thought of you.
You were in my heart,
My love never changed
I still feel the same.

(Jason)
Especially for you
I wanna tell you I was feeling that way too,
And if dreams were wings, you know
I would have flown to you.
To be where you are
(Kylie)
No matter how far.
(Both)
And now that I'm next to you

(Jason)
No more dreaming about tomorrow,
Forget the loneliness and the sorrow.
(Kylie)
I've got to say
(Both)
It's all because of you

And now we're back together, together
I wanna show you my heart is oh so true,
And all the love I have is especially for you.

(Kylie)
Especially for you
I wanna tell you,
You mean all the world to me,
(Jason)
How I'm certain
That our love was meant to be
You changed my life,
(Kylie)
You showed me the way
(Both)
And now that I'm next to you

(Jason)
I've waited long enough to find you
I wanna put all the hurt behind you
(Kylie)
Oh, and I wanna bring out
All the love inside you,

(Both)
Oh and now we're back together, together
I wanna show you my heart is oh so true,
And all the love I have is especially for you.

Instrumental

(Kylie)
You were in my heart
My love never changed.

(Jason)
No more dreaming about tomorrow,
Forget the loneliness and the sorrow.
(Kylie)
I've got to say
(Both)
It's all because of you

And now we're back together, together
I wanna show you my heart is oh so true,
And all the love I have is especially for (you.)
Together, together,
I wanna show you my heart is oh so true,
And all the love I have is especially for (you.)

repeat to fade

6. Hand On Your Heart

Words & Music by Mike Stock, Matt Aitken & Pete Waterman

Put your hand on your heart and tell me,
That we're through, ooh.

Oh, put your hand on your heart,
Hand on your heart.

Well it's one thing to fall in love
But another to make it last.
I thought that we were just beginning,
And now you say we're in the past.
Oh, look me in the eye
And tell me we are really through.
You know it's one thing to say you love me
But another to mean it from the heart.
And if you don't intend to see it through
Why did we ever start?
Oh, I wanna hear you tell me
You don't want my love.

Put your hand on your heart and tell me
It's all over.
I won't believe it till
You put your hand on your heart and tell me
That we're through, ooh
Oh, put your hand on your heart,
Hand on your heart.

They like to talk about forever
But most people never get the chance.
Do you wanna lose our love together,
Do you find a new romance?
Oh, I wanna hear you tell me
You don't want my love.

Put your hand on your heart and tell me
It's all over.
I won't believe it till
You put your hand on your heart and tell me
That we're through, ooh

Put your hand on your heart and tell me
It's all over.
I won't believe it till
You put your hand on your heart and tell me
That we're through, ooh
Put your hand on your heart

Hand on your heart,
(Hand on your heart)
Hand on your heart,
(Hand on your heart)
Hand on your heart...

Oh, look me in the eye
And tell me we are really through

Put your hand on your heart and tell me
It's all over.
I won't believe it till
You put your hand on your heart and tell me
That we're through, ooh

Put your hand on your heart and tell me
It's all over.
I won't believe it till
You put your hand on your heart and tell me
That we're through, ooh...

repeat chorus to fade

7. I Should Be So Lucky

Words & Music by Mike Stock, Matt Aitken & Pete Waterman

In my imagination
There is no complication,
I dream about you all the time.
In my mind a celebration
The sweetest of sensation,
Thinking you could be mine.

In my imagination
There is no hesitation,
We walk together hand in hand
I'm dreaming...
You fell in love with me,
Like I'm in love with you,
But dreaming's all I do
If only they'd come true.

I should be so lucky
Lucky, lucky, lucky
I should be so lucky in love.
I should be so lucky
Lucky, lucky, lucky
I should be so lucky in love.

It's a crazy situation
You always keep me waiting
Because it's only make-believe.
And I would come a-running
To give you all my loving
If one day you would notice me.

My heart is close to breaking
And I can't go on faking
The fantasy that you'll be mine
I'm dreaming...
Like you're in love with me
Like I'm in love with you
But dreaming's all I do
If only they'd come true.

I should be so lucky
Lucky, lucky, lucky
I should be so lucky in love.
I should be so lucky
Lucky, lucky, lucky
I should be so lucky in love.

I should be so lucky,
I should be so lucky
I, I, (I, I)
I should be so lucky,
I should be so lucky
I, I, I, I, I, I, I, I, I, I

Instrumental

In my imagination
There is no hesitation,
We walk together hand in hand
I'm dreaming...
You fell in love with me,
Like I'm in love with you,
But dreaming's all I do
If only they'd come true.

I should be so lucky
(Lucky, lucky, lucky)
I should be so lucky in love.
I should be so lucky
(Lucky, lucky, lucky)
I should be so lucky in love.

repeat to fade

8. Love At First Sight

Words & Music by Kylie Minogue, Richard Stannard,
Julian Gallagher, Ash Howes & Martin Harrington

Thought that I was going crazy,
Just having one of those days yeah.
Didn't know what to do
Then there was you.

And everything went from wrong to right,
And the stars came out
And filled up the sky,
The music you were playing
Really blew my mind,
It was love, at first sight.

'Cause baby when I heard you
For the first time I knew
We were meant to be as one.

Was tired of running out of luck,
Thinking 'bout giving up yeah,
Didn't know what to do
Then there was you.

And everything went from wrong to right,
And the stars came out
And filled up the sky,
The music you were playing
Really blew my mind,
It was love, at first sight.

'Cause baby when I heard you
For the first time I knew
We were meant to be as one.
'Cause baby when I heard you
For the first time I knew
We were meant to be as one.

Instrumental

And everything went from wrong to right
And the stars came out
And filled up the sky
The music you were playing
Really blew my mind
It was love at first sight
Love at first sight,
Love at first sight,
Love, oh it was love, it was love at first sight.

'Cause baby when I heard you
For the first time I knew
We were meant to be as one.
'Cause baby when I heard you
For the first time I knew
We were meant to be as one.

It was love, it was love,
It was love, it was love

repeat to fade

9. On A Night Like This

Words & Music by Brian Rawling, Graham Stack,
Mark Taylor & Steve Torch

(You kiss me, you touch me)

Don't, say, it's like a fantasy
When, you, know this is how it should be.

You kiss me, I'm falling
Can you hear me calling?
You touch me, I want you
Feels like I've always known you.

On a night like this
I wanna stay forever, (stay forever)
On a night like this
Just wanna be together
On a night like this.

Now, I'm, getting closer to you
Hold, me, I just can't be without you.

You kiss me, I'm falling
It's your name I'm calling,
You touch me, I want you
Feels like I've always known you.

On a night like this
I wanna stay forever, (stay forever)
On a night like this
Just wanna be together
On a night like this.

Seems I've known you a lifetime,
Now it's time to make you mine
On a night like this. . .
On a night like this, oh.

You kiss me, I'm falling, you touch me.

On a night like this,
Just wanna be together.

On a night like this
I wanna stay forever, (stay forever)
On a night like this
Just wanna be together
On a night like this.

You kiss me, I'm falling, you touch me.

On a night like this.

to fade

10. **Spinning Around**

Words & Music by Ira Shickman, Osbourne Bingham, Kara Dioguardi & Paula Abdul

Spinning around
Oh

I'm spinnin' around, move out of my way
I know you're feelin' me
'Cause you like it like this,
I'm breakin' it down, I'm not the same
I know you're feelin' me
'Cause you like it like (this.)

Clearin' this house out of joy
That I borrowed
From back in the day,
Threw away my old clothes
Got myself a better wardrobe
I got something to say.
I'm through with the past
Ain't no point in looking back,
The future will be.
And did I forget to mention that
I found a new direction,
And it leads back to me.

I'm spinnin' around, move out of my way
I know you're feelin' me
'Cause you like it like this,
I'm breakin' it down, I'm not the same
I know you're feelin' me 'cause you like it...

The mistakes that I made,
Givin' me the strength
To really believe.
And no matter how I take it
There's no way I'm gonna fake it
'Cause it's gotta be real.
I've got nothin' left to hide
No reason left to fight,
'Cause the truth's given me
A new freedom inside
Gettin' rid of my desire
Do you like what you see?

I'm spinnin' around, move out of my way
I know you're feelin' me
'Cause you like it like this,
I'm breakin' it down, I'm not the same
I know you're feelin' me
'Cause you like it like this.

Ooh. Baby, baby, baby
You know you like it like this.
Oh baby, baby, baby
You know you like it like this
Oh baby, baby, baby...

I'm spinnin' around, move out of my way
I know you're feelin' me
'Cause you like it like this,
I'm breakin' it down, I'm not the same
I know you're feelin' me
'Cause you like it like this.

repeat ad lib to fade

CD Track Listing

1. **Better The Devil You Know**
Stock / Aitken / Waterman
All Boys Music Limited / Mike Stock Publishing Limited / Universal Music Publishing Limited.

2. **Can't Get You Out Of My Head**
Dennis / Davis
EMI Music Publishing Limited / Universal / MCA Music Limited.

3. **Come Into My World**
Dennis / Davis
EMI Music Publishing Limited / Universal / MCA Music Limited.

4. **Confide In Me**
Anderson / Seaman / Barton
BMG Music Publishing Limited / Universal / MCA Music Limited / Complete Music Limited.

5. **Especially For You**
Stock / Aitken / Waterman
All Boys Music Limited / Mike Stock Publishing Limited / Universal Music Publishing Limited.

6. **Hand On Your Heart**
Stock / Aitken / Waterman
All Boys Music Limited / Mike Stock Publishing Limited / Universal Music Publishing Limited.

7. **I Should Be So Lucky**
Stock / Aitken / Waterman
All Boys Music Limited / Mike Stock Publishing Limited / Universal Music Publishing Limited.

8. **Love At First Sight**
Minogue / Stannard / Gallagher / Howes / Harrington
Universal Music Publishing Limited / Sony / ATV Music Publishing (UK) Limited / EMI Music Publishing Limited / The International Music Network Limited.

9. **On A Night Like This**
Rawling / Stack / Taylor / Torch
Rive Droite Music.

10. **Spinning Around**
Shickman / Bingham / Dioguardi / Abdul
EMI Music Publishing Limited / Warner / Chappell Music Limited.

To remove your CD from the plastic sleeve, lift the small lip on the right to break the perforated flap. Replace the disc after use for convenient storage.